Monsoon on the Fingers of God

poems

Sasenarine Persaud

MAWENZI HOUSE

We acknowledge the support of the Canada Council for the Arts for our publishing program. We also acknowledge support from the Government of Ontario through the Ontario Arts Council.

Cover design by Sabrina Pignataro

Cover photo: Wolkenengel565/Wonderful heavy rain shower in the sunshine of springtime or summer enjoy the relaxing nature/Shutterstock

Library and Archives Canada Cataloguing in Publication

Persaud, Sasenarine, 1958-, author
Monsoon on the fingers of God : poems / Sasenarine Persaud.

Issued in print and electronic formats.
ISBN 978-1-988449-31-9 (softcover).—ISBN 978-1-988449-38-8 (HTML)

I. Title.

PS8581.E7495M65 2018 C811'.54 C2018-901341-9
C2018-901342-7

Printed and bound in Canada by Coach House Printing

Mawenzi House Publishers Ltd.
39 Woburn Avenue (B)
Toronto, Ontario M5M 1K5
Canada
www.mawenzihouse.com

Praise for *Love in a Time of Technology:*

"[T]he poet's mastery of the English language is underwritten by ancestral histories and myths. Love is age-old and universal . . . Persaud is a poet of precise language, of the finely-honed meaning . . ." —*Wasafiri*

Praise for *Lantana Strangling Ixora:*

"A diverse and wide-ranging collection of poems . . . explored with his signature wit and skilful mastery of language . . . powerful images of nature are to be found in his accomplished use of metaphor and simile, which often renders the ordinary into something quite extraordinary . . . a finely balanced collection of work which carefully mixes the past with the present without ever resorting to sentimentality or pathos."
—*Wasafiri*

"Beguiling . . . masterly control" —*Muse India*

"Persaud is dauntlessly brainy . . . a bit like reading T.S. Eliot mixed up with Rabindranath Tagore . . . Persaud's poems are unapologetically learned."
—*The Halifax Chronicle Herald*

Praise for *In a Boston Night:*

"[Persaud's] poetry [is] timeless in nature in its discussions of sensuality, love and mourning, but also modern for its interspersion of technology and discussion of contemporary politics. . . refreshingly sensual and realistic."
—Kavita Ramdia, News India Times

"Each poem, held on the tongue, tastes true—he's one of those rare poets who gets the recipe of humanness exactly right"
—*Canadian Literature*

BOOKS BY
SASENARINE PERSAUD

Demerary Telepathy
Between the Dash and the Comma
Dear Death
The Ghost of Bellow's Man
A Surf of Sparrows' Songs
Canada Geese and Apple Chatney
The Hungry Sailor
The Wintering Kundalini
A Writer Like You
In a Boston Night
Lantana Strangling Ixora
Unclosed Entrances
Love in a Time of Technology

CONTENTS

PRELUDE

Old Loves New Loves

You come, tigers in the night
circling embers in our hearts
would ignite in a second—
who can tell? Lessons we never learned
are minds exploding, exploring
for things we could never do
the gulf too wide to leap
across skins. A child uttering
if you drink milk, you will get fair
like a white tiger, a ghost cat, an Asian
feline's eyes mocking the dark—and memory

Karma Mornings

When did you melt into the white-brown
morning mist indentured to the land, into
the fire-flaming cardinal on the paling;
when did you melt like a black racer*
into the rain-cavorting grass and pink
beauties, rain lilies, ringing the wild lawn;
when did I say: I did not need you ever
again the raucous evenings—your sex

* A common Florida rat snake

Cove Park

1

Rain again on the loch below
liner and luxury yacht toys—
is that a submarine on the surface
false alarm, bells ringing
your breasts and lovers who left
no pain on limbs such nakedness
we become used to—in which shire—
still erotic in the circling, waiting

A black dog bounding through building
from master to mistress. Mud and rain.
The ancients didn't wash often
after in the cold, clothes smelling
canine but when we descend
between the covers, black letters
on white pages, pudendum is pudendum.
Evolution, you say, from what

2

We turn and career following
crevasses and water cuts in rocks
kilting the loch, accelerating up steep inclines.
That is the naval base, says the cabbie,
I know, worked there for 10 years: bean counter

The subs are hidden in the mountain—
armaments kept over there, separate.
You don't want an international incident
now, do you? We pull up the closing
ceremonies using a borrowed projector

He who fathered a son with a lesbian, unimportant,
conscious of a referendum; how many times
will Glasgow and Scotland have been excellent
hosts—the best Games ever. Who won the most
medals or the third most doesn't matter

You show the dirty toilets of the Delhi Games
how the Indian Commonwealth Games Chair
was jailed for corruption—and in the end
Robbie Burns' Auld Lang Syne—not quite
as our father singing on Old Year's Night, tears

In our unhidden hearts as we turn off the lights
set the alarm and head down the steep footpath
in the cool, charcoal night for cabins for pods

3

Clambering up the loft after
what did you see? Sun setting
on loch, mountains, hills?

There is that familiar sound in Doric
north north-east a fishing village
overlording an ancient Pict fort
and settlement. Swifts turn on tail tips
plucking insects from the dark
pond. We edge away. Fishermen's
timbers curved in a vessel. Our hearts

Throb like kathakali dancers' toes
and then is gone to Goa, Kanyakumari
all the way up to Delhi, Rajasthan and back
to a Carnatic violin bowed like a cello

The nuclear sub on the surface, now gone.
What if—it is only fifty miles to Glasgow—
an accident? We are a bombing range

For the RAF up north. Drinking in a BBC
bar and missing half the closing—
investigative reporter, sun sinking
on a ship near the loch, jeweled anchors
on ankles, a flute. You do not take off
your shirt to celebrate the passing

Of fishing folk. You sing a Doric hymn.
Deathsong, sipping Scottish tea, birthsong

4

We always have unfinished business—
your mountain or mine—
these highland ducks seeking
constantly under rocks among turmeric
wildflowers and reeds circumscribed
by this pond, this brackish water
that is home, yet we venture out
and take our hearts, Caledonia, take
our souls, Himalaya, trickling down crags.
We always have unfinished business,
Ganga*—your delta or mine

* Ganga is the Indian name for the Ganges River and also the goddess Ganga who (as Shiva was meditating high in the Himalayas) descended to earth in the snow, unto Shiva's head trickling down the mountains to form the Ganga, the river that bears her name. There are many other stories about Ganga and her appearances on earth in the *Mahabharata*.

5

As you walk up the footpath
to the vehicle taking you away,
mountain birches restrain
leaves from muttering
things you didn't do
well, that cut up the peak
you refrained from traversing
that canoe in the shed you didn't
take out in the upland lake
that walk down to the mossed sand,
rock-punctured and black, you couldn't
make knowing you will return and not
turn back lest your heart turn to rock
salt because you're not saying
goodbye goodbye goodbye

Edinburgh

Serving Demerara sugar above Waverley
Station, golden brown like the glazed Tate
& Lyle satchel and your eyes smiling
and moving diners on outside two black-hatted,
black-robed boys pull bags uphill
the Castle top, the Balmoral domes
why Nelson's monument here Scott's
spires and crags and crevices on old stone
buildings all washed in uncreamed coffee—
rain and the creek-black stains everywhere

1 – Through Waverley

How eyes look like sugarcane
juice and spring-green shoots
as we stand on a ledge
off Royal Mile unable to leap

Into a crag below. How
oxygen pumps in chests sound
like trains rolling into Waverley
Station on a windy wet day
dampening clattering wheels

Up a hill down a hill—and why
not simply say uphill downhill—
Starbuck one, Starbucks two
American poets lending names
to coffee houses we pass and cross

Paths all our hearts crying never
Let me go, never let me go

2

In these clouds, we are mists
and there are cities below
Glasgow, or an ancestral village
created from the bogs. In this air
sun sparkles on aluminum and steel
and you could say: The Clearings

We were poor once and over centuries
we had a hut, if you crossed
from the Mainland, you gain a language

You cross from the Mainland
you gain a land. But these are all islands
to strangers. Rain water runs downhill
as you go uphill, through open-tip shoes

On toes we might hold or touch or tongue
tasting a hairy pie or a scone
gives us language, gives us love

3

Threading rings demonstrating the airbus emergency
safety apparatus, metal speaks and air escaping sings
at five, winning a competition in ancient diphthongs
and sibilants crossing with rain and western relatives

How did they arrive on the Irish Isles?
Or was that from, academic, when ancestral lands
were all joined in a pelvic dance, we are straining
to remember it is and isn't a miracle

For forest flames leaping from brown bramble
to dark green palms is no curse for eyes
rain no terror for a pyre intent on reclaiming
bones, only today it is flesh and something more
we're after: one who would be parent spouse actor

4

Hold my arm down the wet close
down this steep incline grimed
at the edges old stones greening
take new breath from souls through soles
cautious in the close, one slip
and we reach that bottom too quickly

Hold my arm as none has
disengaging before you think, uttering
beneath breath, beneath Krishna clouds
and Goberdhan mountain, hold my hand
hold my heart and never let me go

5

Blood congealing in a grandmother's bucket
on the floor. We are consuming black
pudding below the gaze of departed mothers
and fathers, another grandmother shelling
shrimps and you are walking back
with a fisherman's catch: red snapper, ocean
catfish yellowing in a turmeric mixture. Curry
makes anything palatable. I would show
Indian spices, garam masala, ground black
pepper corns even unknowing half her recipes
and straining to catch her voice child-filed

Let him go—and her mother's—we can raise
our children on our own. And she did

After a long day, I measure her scented tobacco
and watch her practiced roll and paper licking.
A lighter clicking, lighting up our eyes as your
laughter in the overcast and rain dripping off
roofs and eaves unto the lizard-green concrete

6

Chlorophyll earing in eyes, but no tinge
you know on lips, no tinge you know
at finger tips, no tint you know on toes—
It was all in eyes, all in tongues, in utterance

7

And I could tell you nothing
of ancestral speech, nothing of Kali's
extended tongue signifying: you are she
divine, supreme controller of all desires

8

Gaelic was Gaelic in Ireland, you said
in Scotland Gaelic is Galic
and some might hear garlic.
Not many in these isles know this

We listen. I have no famous language
to give, no metaphors and fine figures
of speech, frontiers men in the West
shooting straight from the hip—
we want your head and heart and soul
and body—whole we offer but cannot give

9

In a second, I would be SheshaNarayana
serpent god and serpent king kundalini
keeper and guardian: This is tomorrow
and tomorrow and no tomorrow—there is
no other world and space and time
no other world, but this and here and now

10

We are wasting nothing. Not children theatre
not haggis, not the liver of cow
the blood of lamb, not the intestines
of sheep scrubbed and flipped over and scrubbed
and sliced, boiled and fried in coconut fryoil
and spices—a masala making our tongues
water—tripe you would not now taste
except from another's fingers, another's tongue

11

We would go to an island home
ancestral land I'd never visited.
You would be gone, laughing
to be rid of the northern moist, deluge
and now no more. Home is where
the roof leaks, where the ground is sodden
where the road puddles, where drains
overflow, where hearts are flooded, where
pumps work overtime to spread this glow

12

Long hair tucked, or curled short
in this rain who can tell you
are a thousand forms—birthskin
denim, yoga-jeans, wool and cotton
frock, summer-fresh skirt touching ankles

You are everywhere: Princess Garden
Charlotte Square, The Briggait, strolling
along the Clyde and even on Cannongate

13

In the night, it was ratoon and how
to cut cane, planting rows, plantations
we strain to hear the quivering
voice whispering from the grave:
We know, we know, who are buried
here in the moist night, in the crags
and folds of voice, the crevices of flesh

14

You can never bid goodbye
and yet you did—goodbye
and do not turn around in rain

15

Three million pounds for language services
fifteen for TV and the Welsh one hundred
million. In the authors yurt, an Irish moderator
says, "I'm sixty, single and retired with the means
to travel. If water falls on a neighbour's head
if water damages her ceiling and bed, it's only
Money. Replaceable." Laughter. It's in the eyes

A thousand thousand die each year. Six hundred
and we think, Gaelic will die—what is Doric!
Another maths* defeats maths: if you get one
just one new speaker annually, this language
will live as long as humans live. I cannot
name the village from which my father's father's

* In British English, and in most former British colonies, mathematics is abbreviated as maths; and words such as color, neighbor and labor are still spelled with a "u."

father's father's father came. And still, I do not
envy you—grass eyes—and yet we have love
a language we cannot give love until we love

16

Wallet—three credit cards, a license to drive
a couple hundred dollar notes
Bank of Scotland twenty pound bills
a card from the English PEN Director
New Zealand, Ukraine and British
then we see who are paupers, who
princesses—lost somewhere on the flight
from Edinburgh to the Florida flatlands
arriving empty-handed, not empty-headed

17

Mid-thirty, we laugh, no highland man thick
of girth, and strong enough to hold
rappelling ropes down the ledges spiking
birds—hatchlings heaped and boiled
different worlds—and after all the wars
between the clans, how we quartered a stomach
and spiked a head—concealing a memory

Don't ask, don't tell how once
we cut the necks of fowl, plucking feathers
in boiling water, then roasting off ingrown tips
from skin, trimming legs and wings—what
wrong in taking that which pleases
tongue—language, we give you love
love, you give us language

18

Haggis and spices from an Indian
friend. In the bush, the Arawak
dried cassava whiter than skeletal
bone or your neck lit by flashes
in the storm—cassava-bread thin as puri
crisp and warping left and right and high
and low; too much starch is not enough
preparing for the next famine on the pond's
other face 4,000 miles away, when hunting
is uncertain, when game is scarce, when
cowards might well be the wards of cows
afraid of hearts thumping, dancing hooves
in green island pastures, emerald South
American savannahs, rain-rich Florida fields
making a green Atlantic blue in fall light

19

These flowers didn't ask to be cut
and placed in vases, these flowers
didn't ask to be cut and placed
on tables in a ring of fire
along the fence and the undecorated
lawn's page green and blank as our hearts
as we cling to this ocean silence

20

Transparent nails on toes on fingers
on a table's edge coconut crumbs fall
on eyes a land I would give riddled
with tall palms, spreading mango trees

laden in these seasons we can't
now see sun setting on a southern Atlantic
shore, in this rain we would dry the crags
between toe and tongue—the dancing
Shiva's and Kali's deluge off lips
do not stop—singing: let it rain
all afternoon, let it rain all day, all night

21

White elephants raise their trunks
on a wall before us—compressed paperboard
absorbing shadows—you draw the blinds
to keep out the glare beyond Long Loch
and the Florida Gulf, the sun is the same
seduction tipping the horizon. And I can tell you
now how Ganesha gained his elephant head

22

Was Will accurate or taking poetic license
Lady Macbeth naked washing herself
her hands—not all the Scottish waters
erasing murder. Silence from your side
of our pond. My bonnie lies over the ocean
my bonnie lies over the sea, we sang
in a colonial childhood, who the colonizer?

This was once a quiet neighbourhood
beyond the dog-eared fence, and once this sun
sets, it will be again. Did Will cross Hadrian's
Wall? Yet heaven's breath smells wooingly here

On this raindrenched grass sunsplashed after
the shower and greener than iris expanding
in the darkening room you share ancestors—the
extent of charity. You do not share lovers
you know, Lady Macbeth was married twice

23

He held her down, while they murdered
her reputed lover, in turn facing the same
end. His murderer becoming husband
number two or three. She was too young

We bypass the Palace of Holyrood. Blood
and ornate ghosts in towers—the end
caught Elizabeth limping and losing hair,
her head. Raleigh elsewhere. Longevity
a record among monarchy. To spite a son
defying—puritans. Who were the pilgrims

What Princess Papers! It is the other
that matters. You curse London,
the earls of Northumberland and Paris
alliances and Romans and Vikings
and Britannics but never the Celts
or roving Irish, who brought you this thing
you love: languages sourced from elsewhere

24

Startled like a brown thrush in the shrubs
by its own shadow, upright in a bed
of roses, and yet no sweat touches
sheet, or pillowcase. Air-conditioning sees
to this. But whose room, whose house

whose home is this with underwear blinds
filtering streetlight, from whose city? In this
eternal minute, this much we know:
This is my home. This is not my home

25

On Princess Street, on Waterloo Place
you crack the blinds. Light dances
on the Balmoral until 10 pm. On the hill
cannons boom. Men in skirts perform
in the Military Tattoo. Men in skirts
are Balmoral doormen. Cross-dressing
with pride, Alba—progressive your ghosts
walk uphill to Leith; your ghost follows

Without a shoe-sole rustle, a whisper for me
we were no lords of manors, no Bruces
of Bruce, no Balliols, no Marys with French
retinue, or French petticoats, or curved things
tomorrow for breakfast, croissants—pardon
my French—as we follow close in the dark

26

In the Spiegel tent, old men sing.
A woman strums a guitar. Blond
or grey is hard to say. Two girls twist
and sway on the wooden floor.
You're an interloper among the Guardian
Girls. Shop talk. What kind of name is Laura
with a new job, new eyes in the clublight
washed out grey-blue like this morning's sky—
a queer man isn't he, edging in behind to pass
on the left, then gone. Black-suited celebrity

27

We leave quietly in ones or twos.
You hold on, pulling back gently
like uncle Georgie on the cast-net
trying to pull back the evening
staving off tomorrow. Anne in black,
uniform of festival volunteers,
checks the rubbish bins, changes
transparent plastic bags. We need
to see if trash is trash. Design graduate
or architecture. Why? So I can
mingle with the stars. Look! Dust
falls off our fingers. There's nothing
on our tongues except goodnights
you cannot buy in any café in any
country, but in this tendril light
a roaring tent—Tam o' shanter-away away

28

I come to you in rain, fishhawk
I come to you in rain, falcon
eater of boiled and heaped hatchlings
livers and gizzards, sheep's intestines
lamb's blood, buckets on floor
in a grandmother's house where it leaks
on nose, on ears, on eyes, lips, tongues

29

This brighter-than-heaven sunshine
in the early morning lights the rainrich
grass sparkling from last night's showers
finds no parallel except you'd forget
The Clearings: landlords moving peasants
off their land—here, some choice

Florida Creeks and Seminoles transported
to the Midwest appropriating their hammocks
Brando in a whisper: *We live on stolen land*
if you'd forget a race, a tribe disappeared
one million Calusa—artifacts reminding

You have a language, still, the Gaelic
in your face, eyes, off your lips
and curling tongue; and this unenough

The guide expounds on battles
and murdered Scoti, marauding English
an amalgam of the same Britannic
Norman, Viking, Roman on the east—
what is Doric, we ask on a loft
over Long Loch waiting for the submarine

A British nuclear deterrent hidden
in these mountains, to pass—one hundred
or fifty more miles from Glasgow—what if
up north the RAF flattens a field
for bombing practice; we would do it
better ourselves, between tea and the trek

Up the steep path to the main building
a mile, a million years waiting for a taxi
Canadian, how did you find yourself
in these uplands waiting for this world
to pass through your gaze and the audacity
—"poetry doesn't pay the bills"—

to compose a fiction on early Auden nearby
in Helensburg contemplating the Golden Calf
and the valleys of Sodom and asking why
do Hindus worship cows, or Europeans dogs
or pussies—ass the ass—someone whispering
a South American Indian shipwrecked
Cristobal, ah Cristobal sailing westeast
for curry, for spices in a tiny Kilcreggan market
store and post office open on a bank holiday

How did you find yourself naked
on a cover, in the much praised pages
of a thin volume, your heart raw, vulva aching
publicly more eloquent than any penis
rising like the wind outside on the loch

On paper-white birches bending
and flaying the air, the moment passing
The Games over, Lulu with face and tummy
tuck belting out a comeback hit not quite close
to, "To Sir With Love" and the icon's

Breaking voice on "Caledonia"—what names
you have like my thousand names for Vishnu:
Lanark or Clydesdale or none; the Outer
Islands—the Hebrides—we are descending

A wet path single file: Andrew and his Dundee
girl in front—A torch! A torch! A cow! A Horse!
Smartphone torchapps illuminating the asphalt night.
Look out for cowpats! Someone yells too late

Where are the Gopis, where their herds
their milk tomorrow in the village market
Emily hitting on an artist, the smallest squished
automatically in centreback, the pickup has
manual transmission, better for steep hills

Better for—I can teach you how to shift—
love; they head off in the afternoon sunshine
to plan tonight, or tomorrow away
from sticky ears—what can we tell

Your lover, the black dog bounding between
master and ward and your mountain hospitality
the canine dancing out the door
as you depart: I will not come back

I will not return for the unfresh underwear
or the lemon-striped towel, favoured—best—
grass, buds, butterflies, eyes, eyes, eyes—
I will not return for pasteurised orange juice
or Scottish cheddar—pure upland milk
mist concealing a ring of wireless transmission

Towers zapping us in this wilderness
A cancer we cannot see, you quip: do everything
in moderation except for this fire in our fingers
in our minds, all expression—even vulvatasting
penistongue—some form of vanity—we pour

Our limbs on paper, on keyboard our
hearts and soul from the kettle
into teacups and hope your sip satiates
knowing we will never revisit this space

30

Sun darts through portholes
on the loft two pillows set for strangers
and stranger sights when clouds part
we cannot remember the opaque between
only light in the valley below
moisture gleaming like jello as wind
falls, as we climb down the ladder
always tea. There is no tomorrow
the Carvaka* says, no other world but this

31

On the drive to Inverness, Macbeth appears
and lipred Macbheatha's wife stooping. Another
new word: Plockton. Soulopened world
after leaving Mr Mackenzie, Rhys's heroine reading
and drinking in a dark Parisian room dreaming
of sunshine on banana suckers reflecting rainbows
and Rhys' West Indian childhood. Dali's village
appearing on every painting—look, says the Guide

32

In midmorning, a beetle so loud
you think decibels and ringing eardrums
and traffic made insignificant by a bird
you haven't heard in years like love

* One of the more than half a dozen systems of Indian philosophy.

you would know nonspecifically anywhere
"You cannot divide a samosa equally
between two friends." Maybe samosas weren't
meant to be shared. The quivering leafshadows
on the fence will never hear you say again
I will in English or Sanskrit or any language
silence is a word, the beetle has ceased
rattling the morning—and the bird is gone

33 – Exiles: Americans in Edinburgh

Hands hold hands lingering on fingers slowly
up to elbows, our long noses meeting—
from where you say? I didn't, yet, sitting
near a heater on Europe's western edge
this yurt from the steppes smothering and yet

Hesse travelling in our eyes and fingertips
on forearm on the American Dream jaded—
West Milford, New Jersey or somewhere
in Boston, the declaration: we love we love not

It was time for me to strike out on my own.
I will be fine among the Williamses—
One Roger Williams was on the Mayflower
or some such vessel, finally founding Providence.
In August sunshine, alternating with rain on Sunday
we are new to mousetown scents taken to Florida

We will never make it to India, you say
we are different—our heart is painted Gaelic
and yours Britannic, our liver Scoti, yours Sanskrit
we know the bile of a thousand years. Muslims
dreaming of Mecca—except when we touch arms
and our eyes sing: never let me go, never let me go

34 – Indian Doctor Loosens Her Hair after Operation

The cars sleep at noon in the heat
Spain takes siestas—no wonder their economy
tanks! the feudal master is Percy—who knows
why a great-grand uncle in Campbellville
was called "Percy"—a Duke in Northumberland
or Raja of Jaipur, or CEO of Mizuho Bank Inc.—
But we laugh because you are an engineer of limbs
hearts and organs and yours was a successful surgery
and because we are an ancient Sunya—zero
mirage in midday heat—nothing nothing nothing

35

Postcards unenhanced. Tourbooks accurate
in reconciling local to stranger, tourist
in this ancient land your tongue travelling
across seas—forked pathways, forked utterances
sweet as our morning coffee watching mist
lift from the loch then cover us again
in rain—pani re pani tera rang kisa*—
celebrating monsoon on Mumbai celluloid.
But then we are resting eyes on eyes
and there are no tourists and locals
no guide, no guided as the rain ceases

36

Taking to hills lined with white coatings
along ridges, there is a mist concealing
peaks we did not reach descending to water
along Atlantic shores—blue waves

* Rain, what is your colour (a song from the 1972 movie, *Shor*)

moss-tinged in your eyes left on steep slopes
souls merging with timberland and canines
frolicking in snow limbs, neck an avalanche—
it was goodbye, then, before goodnight, before
good morning losing to utterance, to language

37

Walking down a narrow path in the dark
there is laughter ahead. *Watch your foot.*
You don't want to twist an ankle,
or step in cow droppings. You hear a step
behind and turn, flipping the minilight
a phosphorus glow on stone where cattle
wandered in the day, pinprick on a highland
trail. Maybe an ancient ghost. Cow dung smells
the same everywhere: on a Scots hill, in pastures
north of Toronto, on South American flatlands
we daubed bottomhouses and firesides with gobar*—
Please hook the latch and lock the fence. One last
look behind. Entering facing outwards
spirits couldn't follow you in. And yet, later,
under the comforter there is your touch
like green leaves in wind, anonymous

* Indian word for cow-droppings

38

We traversed oceans on vessels crafted
on the Thames and Clyde—those who passed
pressed overboard, shark food. Indian Ocean
or Atlantic still one Kala Pani, one blackwater
like the Clyde's spattered with bird discards

Three months* tidedancing and troughswaying
innards on mountain planks, land on waves
an island and yet, The Main. Our journey wasn't
a day like today's riding a vessel over peaks
and lakes and ancient histories and languages

We focus one eye on the past: painted "barbarians"—
Skyblue is vision's trick; it is all kala—unlit—
except reflections from distant suns twinkling like
Raghu's eyes—Hadrian's Wall, Roman steel or Norman
red with sunset's songs on clouds leaching into soil
ignoring longboats, courting the French—Liberty

Equality Fraternity and a guillotine—where was Normandy.

Not in your grassgreen eyes, not in Dublin's Gaelic
different from Scoti Gaelic. Cousins and yet we forget
pupil colours are honey in rain leaching
down cobblestones on The Mile where inhabitants
once threw waste into gullies occupied by Waverley
platforms meeting and parting without hello-goodbye

* The time it took ships to travel from India to the West Indies, bringing Indentured Indian immigrants to work the sugar plantation in the 19th century.

39

Someone points at a black thing rising
from the loch. Monster. We snap pictures
from a moving pickup. Submariners within
sit on nuclear fission. Shiva, someone laughs,
in his dance within fire rings, flame around
zero. Deathcircle. Photos from phonecameras

Before the black vessel is gone—polls trickle in
You see one? Yes, ahead, in this quiet morning
walking up a hill which may be mountain
passing tarfaced sheep. If there were dog's
cousin, here, we would hear bleatings
in Glasgow, see blood on grass, innards

Stretched on trails. Wild wolves reintroduced
in the mountains must live. You say
in Gaelic, made up for the camera: The wolf
belongs here—I give you my neck
but you, strangers, nothing—Alba Alba. Out.

40 – Usha

Usha*: I am this dawn tweeting
wrens high in slash pines, I am
morning mist on scrub and flatwoods
curtained against hardwood hammocks

I am the beards on oaks, yogis'
hair, or desert caliphs come to cities
sowing dissension, I am this sudden flicker
a yolk peeping over mountained treeline
over Loch Long Loch Ness and loch less
I am this instant florescent
transitioning to day and soon gone

* In ancient Vedic/Sanskrit literature Usha is the dawn; in some of the finest poetry, one of the most extraordinary things is how in the midst of, and intertwined with, the deepest philosophical discourses are these seemingly spontaneous songs to nature. Usha is also a feminine name.

41 – Referendum

Skyfilled eyes in sunshine yet it pours
white crosses on your shoulders saltires
saltires saltires. The French peering
over the Atlantic from Canada—Quebec

Skyfilled Fleur-de-lys flapping from antennas
in Florida—and fists. At sixteen we are wise
beyond Holyrood and Westminster
wise beyond septuagenarians. Loaded dice.

You do believe in reincarnation, do you not
love toast in eyes, or emerald pastures
in September rains sputtering like clogged motors

Seafoam from your window—it doesn't matter
in this rain, who said no—waving
palm fronds are all the flags we have to offer
all the flags we need

42

There is an ache in heart
you cannot see palm fronds waving
in morning sunshine limbs calling
crying for laughter in rearing leaflets colts
and calves prancing in wind and pasture
a lone hole in heart you cannot see

43

Weeks of southern heat and then
this morning, rain. Drips from eves heard unseen.
We've slept too much, too long an alarm

failing down a slippery close, not body
clocks, but biorhythm—touch elbow touch arm
touch heart touch soul. Demerara sugar
in stone cities tearing pouches to sweeten tea
or was that bitter coffee? We should have shared
a taxi, we should have gone to Leith

44 – Roma in Edinburgh

Roma, gypsy, India-ink dark
as the drizzle-wet grime-stone
Scott memorial across the flowered Princess
Gardens. We see great-grandmother—Nani—
in your face, cheekbones. Is there a magnet
in your eyes, skin? Tourists dropping coins in a bowl.
Or your bandaged leg, flourwhitefresh wrapped
amputee—in the drizzle? We turn, relieving
pockets of pound coins and guilt unexpressed
for being well, for touring legs. How could you
make this trek from Rajasthan or UP? How could I?

Except in a language we share with the world—
yogayogayoga—through Anglo-Saxon cousins
Sanskrit; or these numbers on streets and hotels
storefront markers, Hindu Numerals
Arabs borrowed from India—zero-invented
decimal system, Demerara sugar humbled
in your clasped palms—namaskar—shamed

On a wet pave, in a basement cafeteria
proclaiming we use only British pork, British duck
British fowl, British sheep grey on a white wall
or later in brilliant afternoon sunshine, on a damp lawn
Nani's eyes etched in my head as we talk dinner
weather and whatever else you do not mention—desire—
in Australian and Scots and how-do-you compute
British-Guianese-Guyanese-Canadian-American-Indian

45 – Puddles

And there it was, leaking. Presumably the radiator
a drop, a pink spot on blue concrete
skies closing fast, another pink spot
on the north face of England
importing stout, frothy Guinness, a language
you call your own to the west, American
infused with Ebonics, or Northumbria
rain-green fields spotted with black-faced sheep
calling itself Scoti and in a wink flying off
to Jamaica. We should honour the slaves
whose sweat built a Glasgow plantation house:
a museum a museum! There is a puddle
on the pavement below Edinburgh castle
on this blue concrete another, pink lips. Radiator
emptying quickly in December, the summer
gone in the sudden cold—mailboxempty silence

46 – The Scott Monument

Water drips down the Scott Monument
down crevasses in grey stone gone black
with accretions—will this rain never stop
until we're gone—the tip a wicked point
not nib, not sword yet that, too. Shiva, we think
a lingum, a lingum city pricking sky
pricking eyes. Gloucester standing on a precipice
head tilted down. We have sight but cannot see
the sign in the airport lounge, a smile erasing
all our pasts—even black stone, even rain—
and a city that honours its writers

47

A lone African orchid nodding
under eves as drops strike
the stalk's long stem curved—
a giraffe's neck listening to rain's palaver
with concrete and loose yard tiles
fired in a foreign kiln is my winter's
downpour as cool as your summer
feet moist in the slope downhill
alleycats crossing Waverley
early Alzheimer's loss of memory

48 – Approaching Day's End

Plunking down your keys, bag
a rattle, pigments from ancient trees
in South America, musk from African
animals, hues from Asian soils—the earth
the heavy earth we release from shoulders
and the work we leave behind and bring
to dinner—cosmetics cracking

In a smile and a deluge of words
silent in a sitcom's laughter travelling
far and fast over hardwood floors
unruffled by the Atlantic's roar

What Caribbean sea, what Mexican Gulf
or Columbian mountain top Maria
Martha Angela we are imbibing coffee
instead of cocaine, pit stop among computer
wheelfans whirring all day and plunking
down keys bags a shak-shak and reaching

For remotes, this control controlling—
we haven't lost the art of speaking
just the energy, the will—memory of love

49 – A Sheep's Life

Two legs hitched up to bottomhouse
ceiling exposing pink-tinged throat.
In the dawn a crimson drip
on clouds and into enamel basins

By noon intestines scrubbed
in and out under the standpipe
wetting us as now washing
and scrubbing like Macbeth's wife

Bunjal* tripe and rum, wasting nothing
north of south and north of north
rolling pastures and rain running
down the Royal Mile we might have

Remained one more day to see you
cleanse your hands, Macbeatha's spouse
bringing us back youth's fire or love or
a time we wasted nothing except a sheep's life

* Bunjal—a dry, curry dish

50 – Accidents: Mother and Sons

Pedaling backwards on the stationary bike
leaned against a post in the bottomhouse
we are sailing over oceans, words chiming—
we would come to know later—like brass jhaals*
anticipating a chowtal's** crescendo, wheels touching

Tarmac, flaps up, flaps down brakes screaming
in a snowpadded night the cassette still
running a raga, the Chrysler-stamped VW Rabbit
stopping in a snowbank and steel guardrail in heaven

You are thinking—it could never be hell—
and, yet, we pedal backwards at the top
of the railway embankment in the drizzle
hurrying to get the baby home before the deluge

Wheels slipping on wet train tracks. You have fallen
at the top mommy—goddess and queen rani ma—
the cycle moving again, I on the carrier seat behind
gliding through rain; but looking back
you never got up, you never got up from that fall

* Jhaals—cymbals

** chowtal—both a taal in Indian classical music and, here, the folk version associated with Phagwah/Holi in India's North East, popular in Guyana, Trinidad, Jamaica, Surinam, Fiji and other countries of the oldest Indian diaspora. The chowtal's crescendo is, arguably, the most powerful in any form of music.

51 – Head Cover

On a brown paper bag, pen freewheeling
on your bicycle, mommy, we cross seas
in the donut shop, stick men running—
"America runs on Dunkin"—stick women
stepping on the toilet door
from a German inventor's fingers
figures designed for forgotten Olympics

Orange walls, orange socks—the South
the South defrocking winter maples
after coy lipstick leaves falling later
and later after we add global warming—
desert palms from every continent
dwarf robellini queen palms all in front

The Public Library waving to Main Street
traffic circling the Cenotaph
after all these years and still no king no god
in this secular space except for a cashier

Smiling under black headcloth designed,
once, to keep Arabian sands from hair—
why do fathers husbands brothers nephews
never wear hijab. Do not ask too many questions,
Gargi,* lest your head burst. We pass plastic

* Gargi was a famous female scholar and philosopher during the Vedic period of around 700 BCE. She participated in several dialogues/debates notably with the great sage and rishi, Yajnavalkya. In one such debate, recorded in the *Upanishads*, she asks a series of questions, which Yajnavalkya answers and adds: Do not ask too many questions, O Gargi, lest you head burst. This is based on Radhkrishnan's translation. There are other slightly different translations of Yajnavalkya's caution, at which Gargi pauses. It is not the end of their discourse, as some modern critics suggest in order to support a particular polemic. Gargi follows up saying she will ask two more

touching fingers taking and giving
throb of heart, skin, flesh, soul—this thing
that has no colour no region no clothcover

52 – On Autumn Leaves

We are hopping on autumn leaves
thick as a duvet infused with tandav—
Shiva's dance dissolving and recreating
time and space and matter

Toronto, a far way from that first
fire, rubbing sticks because some
keen observer—no doubt a poet, or artist
although you will say a scientist—

Observed lightening striking dead wood
rotting twigs on an ancient wildlife trail
leaping and twirling ablaze with sound
and marigold yellow-vermillion flames—

Tandav—our feet pattering bauxite brown
leaves once green and orchestrating wind
how to spin ragas on the insulated earth
fire in toes unsheathed on sugarbrown sheets

---

questions on the ultimate reality. And she does. Yajnavalkya's answers are rich and deep and beautiful as is their entire discourse, and, as is the bulk of the *Upanishads*, which contain some of the finest poetry recorded.

53 – Unpainted

We never painted the house
in 1964 or even in '67—greenheart
cured in equatorial sun mellowing
like aged oak casks imported
from England might well have originated

Elsewhere in the isles—Scotland
or Wales or Ireland, it was all the same:
England. Growing up under the Union Jack
the beanstalk running into an American

Heaven—Hollywood's short and stout and
long, thin duo unknowing the bean was a bora*
vine arriving labouriously through Persian
translations—and wandering Jews—of India

commas and full stops unenough
for the longest Sanskrit words
runonphrases and thoughts and Irish
imitation or a Greek Ulysses
Joyce dreaming up a fable in the south
this south Faulkner said
we are still searching for a period

When Radio Demerara was across
High Street and Parliament Buildings,
gifted by British administrators, around
the corner we'd browse or borrow
or buy in coppers bearing the heads

* Bora—Indian long bean. A few scholars have noted that Jack and the Beanstalk is an adaptation of an Indian story—the bean vine in the story being the Indian long bean known as bora, or bodi

Of old King George or young Elizabeth
a cent being one cent and smaller
than a penny—two cents—unAmerican
Elliot transforming wastelands and murders
in cathedrals and journeying eastwards

Or north Daredevil's eyes behind head
the Phantom, or a tallbuilding crawler
or super Kent not some county cricket team
in the English league white trousers, white
shirts on Bourda Green Dutch and

English mixing easily on a South American
coast white houses reminiscent of Holland
except ours unpainted before mommy
passed—intransigent or economics—
British Guiana dollars and cents

Daddy uncaring after her death a blessing—
no lead paint, just scents of seasalt Trades
bouncing off the Atlantic, rainmoist air
and the fragrance of Chinese plums released
by feasting blue-sakies, parrots and kiskadees

54 – Tiger Tiger

—for Shivnarine Chanderpaul—former West Indies cricket captain

Toes clutching sand on ocean's edge
canefield brown with Brazilian condiments—
silt from the Amazon—stumps in saltwater

Left-handed Shiv or right-handed
Shiva, I'm dancing one-legged at creases
in fire, even with a floating bone

In my foot—no matter, I born
to play ball like Hanuman swallowing
sun for a fruit, *Chalisa** at forty is forty

Peers in pavilions drinking whiskey and rum
I have no equal but the Bengal cat's
waiting at land's end for tossed spheres

Stitched in leather; no hook on the floor
no bottoms on dust, no gazellelike grace
gliding over grass, no elephant trunk

* The *Hanuman Chalisa*, a composition in forty verses summarizing and celebrating the life of Hanuman, was written by the great 16th Century poet, playwright and saint, Tulsidas, who also composed-rewrote the Sanskrit epic, the *Ramayana* in Hindi. The *Chalisa* is sung at pujas in homes and in temples in India and in the Indian diaspora in the West Indies and elsewhere. Many know the entire forty verses by heart. There are several contemporary recordings available including renditions based on ragas. The *Chalisa* is a celebration of grace, strength and endurance. In 2015, due in part to the race politics of the West Indies selectors, Chanderpaul, then 41 and still a great batsman, was not selected for the West Indies cricket team. He subsequently announced his retirement from Test Cricket. Chanderpaul is the holder of several world records in Test Cricket and widely recognized as one of the all-time greats.

Swilling and skirting water on an ocean's
edge, I'm tiger stalking cork ensconced in
leather, tiger striking Wisden with willow.

55 – England

On Tweed's stripe, we disembark
leaving behind a loud "Welcome to Scotland!"
Not turning back. Not once. "I will let you
walk into England," said the Scots driver-guide,
"Look at our sign. Look at theirs!"

From what should be Scottish soil—hurt
disguised as pride and North Sea oil—
nothing on the other side. Leaves, grass, spires
and chimneys. Cameras searching river and bank

We are German American Spanish Chinese—
looking for a mythic land. Dragon and dragon
slayer. Cricket's hallowed grounds. Grandfather
in Bowler hat and tie and jacket—khaki not tweed
how IndianWestIndianEnglish can you get
posing at the hospital gate: English jurisprudence

Robin Hood, Nelson, Morris Oxfords, Vauxhalls,
Minis, a Bentley in the museum, marmite, willow
and the wrath of queen of king, young Winston
charging in a foreign war, Byron, Keats, Bronte

The river calm until midway, someone points to
a repressed stone block sitting on a brick wall
a tiny red cross on a white face engraved in India
ink: *England*. A butterfly sign we could never miss
in a hundred years or two hearts fluttering

Like camera shutters we know this place's
Empire of souls—O Victoria!—mothertongueland

56

First, the lined exercise books bore a monarch's head
crowned and coiffured—Elizabeth's—behind
multiplication tables, measures in inches feet yards
furlongs miles—how far we've come. A world converted

In Toronto: metric. The French ruled in the burial ground.
Le Repentir, an old plantation sectioned and quartered
Catholic, Hindu, Muslim, Protestant—where did the Dutch
inter their dead so far from home—Dutchwoman ghost
riding horse on backdams around old overseer houses

Sheik, living near Sophia koker,* peed on a cheese-and-bread
tree: *Dutch lady ghost slap me unconscious! True. True.*
Lucky watchman see. Pausing. We shivered in Campbellville
Government School, wet and cold, rain pounding
the tall upturned V roof, Bata yachting boots—cheapest

Footwear—wet. Half our class absent. No pound
shilling pence, no hundredweight, pounds, ounces
no Royal Readers, no boy sticking his arm in a hole
in a cracked Polder all night preventing the North Sea
flooding his village. A hero, a hero! Crossing another border

We finally found pints again. Dumping the British
in Boston, in Kew Gardens, Queens, New York
traversing the BQE—that Brooklyn *Queens* Expressway:
Exceptionalism. The next lined notebooks were lost.
What happened Rafique? It was an unfair burden to lug

* Koker: the Dutch word for sluice, still used in Guyana. The Dutch were the first Europeans to settle in Guyana from around the end of the 15th Century.

Our fear around the world on paper. A fountain pen nib's
an arrow with poisoned tip. What did the Warraus
or Wapishanas or Makushi or Wai Wai use? Arapaimas
and boars stunned in a minute. But what is metric time?
The internet we say—if all computers died, if no smartphone
could find electricity, or a virus from Anonymous
in Shanghai or a meteor obliterated all electronics

Even with a stone, or a broken tusk dipped in blood
would we still ink our names on an inch of eternity

57 – Fisherman Returning

Covered in makeshift plastic
coats pelted with rain, we throttle
the outboard. The river stilled
and flattened like hammered zinc
sheets. We return empty handed

Our nets not deployed in the Atlantic
and what do you see under Stabroek's
shaded wharf stilled in this river's
mouth opened wide like packu*—

A longing somewhere under the Union
Jack—My bonnie lies over the ocean
My bonnie lies over the seas—in sun
tomorrow, we will again trawl ocean

Today we're wet like your Britain
and your feline-rearing back flying
a Saltire and welcoming Syrians—
not the English, Potter, your language

* Pacu—A fish found in South American rivers

58 – Confluence

Sitting on grass on sand on beach
vines overgrowing the old Dutch wall
a thousand kites sparkling and singing
and all we ever wanted—and got—
sunshine on silted water, wind curling
ocean, heads on lap on a Demerara leg

On our left the State's Warehouse
British built for HM's colonial Customs
an anachronism if the Scots could do
it over again—we came from the Emerald
Isles. Fantasy. This Gaelic our eyes mimic
is not native to India only

Artificers show that which cries
for son: the portholes in concrete walls
through which pour sunbeams on steel
cages freezing our hearts or how a head—
oiled hair—fits on a skirted pudendum

Perched on grass on sand on ocean
edge, vines on a shellencrusted wall
kite tails curling and singing
come back to me my love come back
to me my confluence come back to me my city

59 – Cove Park

Overlooking the Loch, we curl
like snake charmers to this music
from the Indies. You say chutney
I say chatney laughing a Guyaneseness
that isn't Black British. Columbus
would have been stuck here in the raining
in the wet in the Indian music's wedge

It is not enough in some pre-history
to sing like sakie-winkies, to chatter
like parrots—tuti-nama—we are not uncontent
with Mittelholzer's flute. Silence descends
and keyboards clatter. You could sleep
in a chair—you have on jute bags

On greenheart floors. No way to treat a rishi.
We cell, we text one coming from the Games
in this strange land, we aren't strangers
heritage more than genes, more than this liquid

Falling from clouds swept eastwards
across the Atlantic. We reverse the Trades
opening the bag when Odysseus sleeps—
none will make it home but he who left
his seed behind—grown son, Penelope

A Homer fiction, a men's tale. No woman
but these mountains. I am Shiva I am
Shiva on yonder peak I will descend
tasting mango blossoms—Buxton English
and this spice's peregrinations from our Indies

Heritage more than genes thicker than blood
this Queen's language, masala and mustard oil
in chipped green mango, when Rama returns—
no Homer fiction—to northern mountains

SECTION 2

60 – Tethered Dog Outside Coffee Shop in Alnwick

You pause, coffee eyes rotating head
seeking that mistress who would leave me
tethered to a post. This far south the Scots
are coming again to Northumbria. An economy
in tourist dollars. Castle walls to attend—

How to conceal an army between hillocks.
Which blood-letting is justified in valleys

What is the Gita? asks a question under
your arm. I have time to mull that past
while you accost my mistress in Costa*
sipping coffee from a bowl. Summer heat
summer shade. Tied to a pole, no bitch
in sight. We are dogs, brother, dogs I tell you.

* Costa—a coffee chain in the UK and sponsor of the annual UK Costa Book Awards

61 – Through Waverley Station

Rain igniting the Cove pond
elicits calm peddling from ducks
returns in lightening flashes
but how do we cross Waverley?

On a high bridge, umbrellas dripping
in our faces dirty water soiling toes
open to a strange summer? Connecting
south bank to north in a gulley—
through the sheltered station—
forgetting you despise that Lord's game:
cricket—balls clacking on bats like train
wheels on steel rails is also mine. Lost
comparison. Lost companion comparison

Drizzle following us down the steep
close, green along the edges, seen
only in this Celtic Main or Isles
of Lewis, isles beyond tongue
like Hanuman slipping through ear
and mouth. Ah Bostonian, Southie
your missing "r" in garlic—
this language we speak, strange scripts
words at stations, returning to "Edinboro"

Understanding, Kali, love is your tongue
red heart in mouth—Edinboro in Edinburgh

I would go back, but can't walking instead
in this sky, in this wet, hot closeness
of the crowd, I can't pretend to sing a raga
to your island rain today—give me sun
give me sun give me sun give me sun

62 – Broomsticks at Alnwick Castle

Tweens and toddlers lining up outside
this castle wall listening intently:
how to play a game of fools on broomsticks
on velvet grass and rolling plains in August
sunshine, what must this be like
in winter, northern outpost of realm

A watch, a sentry walking battlements
in a cold guard hut crouched around embers
in a banshee wind waking the dark
listening for barbarians calling in strange tongues

Instructor to children clutching broomsticks—
this is how you play the game of good witches
how you chase a golden ball lofted in the sky
with its own engine and life—430 million copies
no longer fiction, Homer. I waited for them to fly

In the shade of an English elm in the still
British countryside, I waited for kids to mount
broomsticks and take off into the sky.
I waited for tourists alighting from coaches
unloading cars and accents from London
and Berlin and Bihar; Valmiki, I waited
for Tukaram and Tulsi. I waited for Rama
to fly into this green English countryside
for tweens straddling witch-brooms to fly

Chalkboard

Chalk dust flying off blackboards.
When what where and the duster
laden—if you sit in front and volunteered
or if you were tall enough to erase
everything your teachers said, wrote

Horace on Poetry

It might have been attempted
or even accomplished
but we had never seen it done;
how do you paint the throb
of a heart, or flickering leaves
signaling a passing hurricane
the thrum of vina strings
ignited by Saraswatie's fingers?
Horace's the pronouncement
of a colonialist: "Poetry should
Reproduce the qualities of painting."

Egret

The bird was just searching
for food not metaphors—
or taking rest from a day's flight

It was dusk after all and its ancestors
who might have crossed the Middle
Passage, crossed the Kala Pani on flotsam
or a ship's mast long forgotten

We freight this flying feather pen
with a history we cannot forget Dutch
ghosts or jumbies prowling the night—

No wonder the bird takes fright at dark
and huddles in colonies—unshackle
this gauling Mr playwright-painter
let it fly off your canvas tomorrow
into our blue-domed temple into indigo light

Lost

A thief come with technology
to usurp meaning; you can twitter
all night and not make a song
or hear a sparrow or wren

You can surf all day
and never feel a weed washed
up ashore or sand in your toes

Where are you, you said,
I am a pillar of salt
I may last a thousand years
or none, melting in rain today.

Master Batsman

When Shiv* made his debut, stroking grammar
to the boundary, there were still rest days in Test
Cricket, you say, Englishman "the crab" shuffles—
the best you can do, aging colonialists—"obdurate"—
who made this language what it is: calypso

You know, reggae, but not chatney,** not taan***
or a West Indian pooknee**** igniting embers
in a fireside. Sherrigas bite faster than a blink—
you say like a washed up writing school poet
"dull as a dishwasher." A Euro-US alliance.

Do not be fooled by a cat's easy gait
heading for water at dusk, or dinner, bat's repast
another century, where glasses are tinted
and made of Lord's sand, where it is acceptable
to mistake tiger for crab and diamond for dishwasher

"Thank you, sir," we say, antiglare under eyes
we do not thumb our noses, your majesties
royal tons yesterday are, still, royal tons tomorrow

* Shivnarine Chanderpaul, West Indies batsman and former captain of the West Indies team. Holder of several world records. Shiv is also an abbreviation for Shiva.
** Chatney—Indian pickle/condiment and also a fast-paced Indian based music of the West Indies (particularly Trinidad) and South America (Guyana and Surinam), based on the taans of India.
*** Taans—a fast, powerful, rhythmic form of classical Indian singing and music
**** Pooknee—a narrow cylindrical tube, or pipe, used to blow on embers to start a fire

Monsoon on the Fingers of God

(Ravi Shankar 1920-2012)

Forgetting the guru's daughter
or the first or second loves—
reporters seeking out sex and scandal—
third or fifth affairs or ragas; Monterey

Or Woodstock hippies, not crazies,
now, setting an instrument on fire
burning a hand of god, forget

Estranged and unestranged offspring
loved unloved, forget all but this thing
lotused from Saraswattie's vina*
teardrops or raindrops

Monsoon on the fingers of god

* Vina—The oldest known and depicted Indian stringed instrument, and probably the oldest known stringed musical instrument in the world, not dissimilar to the sitar in shape; the oldest precursor of the sitar

This Life

We will take from this lie
a mockingbird imitating a thrush
in the Indian orchid's shade
a wren in the rainrich grass
sparkling stars for a hungry sun
bulbs blooming pink and white opening
to the sky purple bora flowers about to fruit
a lone dwarf rose's red wine
a blue jay strumming the cypress swamp
and your screen, your page, your heart

Memoir: Mother of My Mothers

Ah, Mr Walcott, four years after
Forty-Acres, after we cried
some in joy and some in rage
and the world said: America
you're truly great, truly

Had we gathered those million
tears we'd have had a new sea
as sparkling as dew on dasheen leaves.

Ice caps still melt.

The oceans still rise. The Midwest
still plunged in drought
the economy a fish in a castnet
being hauled ashore. It wasn't me

It wasn't me. But if you give me another
term, I will give you The Great American
Memoir: Mother of my mother's mother.

And some would nod: Mai, Mai, Mai.*

* Mai—Hindi-Bhojpuri for mother. 'Mai, Mai, Mai' is also a story in *Jahaji: An Anthology of Indo-Caribbean Short Stories*

Soul

Like sea, you say
salt and rank and
another day, weeds.
It is not wind
we smell but sea
a breeze apprehended
in dust swirling
in trees gyrating
in rearing breakers
debris twisted from barns
one understood
only through another.

Mind

If mind is all that remains
when body wilts like a Formosa
Azalea in the summer heat
let me not be like memory's toy
tossed between what was
and what might have been, if mind
is all that remains at days' end
let me be fixed in the thrilling
mockingbirds rocking live oaks
or grackles plucking lovebugs
in union on the lawn, or smiles
of those present—if, indeed, there are
any present mouthing, goodbye you f--k
see you on the other side—eyes
responding—if there is another side

White Butterfly

Like that year crickets rend the air
and sliver-bait fish clung to hooks—
fine-pins heated and bent and tied
to limber branch-rods—pasting
flour in palms as we knelt or lay
on stomachs on the banks of Fortyfeet
among daisies and wildflowers
disturbing South American relatives
to catch fish, two, three dozens by noon

Like that year mommy died—who cared
for such adult things as the company
of cousins as distraction—winged wonders
on canna lilies on marigolds and coleus
you come again, tiny-dancing over fence
catwalking and gyrating in my garden

Leaves

Brown leaves rattling a long walkway
in a cool dusk is music in our steps
somewhere along the lake and a roaring
falls' fine mist enveloping faces

How do you think of this time? No babies' cries
child no child, daughter no daughter
sun no son twinkling from an old fort's battlements
fingers in pockets fishing for warmth, leaves

Rattling a maracas from South America
flamenco dancers from Spain or north India—
do you think how love stretched nerves and eyes
to distraction, I scrambling at froth
on the windwhipped water and sunshine
the morning after, blue skies. Our suitcases packed

We will end this tryst with the past. I did not
despise you then and do not now. Mist this morning
does not prevent us seeing: we did not love ourselves
enough to love each other's flaws, or was that only I

Rain

Gulf breeze bringing derby-hoofed drops
on the Floridaroom roof. The Indian orchid
waving like an inebriate football fan
in today's European cup final, a German
girl hoisting an orange and black musketeer hat

The Chancellor is our mascot. We shiver as if
in a winter chill. Fowl-thieves chose rainy
nights to disguise their breaking in, the muted
squawking hens drowned out in the thunder
on metal—those corrugated zinc sheets and these
flat white panels made from the same material

Campbellville

Catching the tossed towel,
we head for water
and you are singing, "My bonnie lies
over the ocean, my bonnie lies over the sea"
mist condensing on the shower door
glass reflecting cane-juice green in your eyes.

You said: *We are connected, you know.*
This south, your south. My ancestors
are Scots. Scotch Bonnet is a South American pepper.
We are laughing in the live-oak-filtered dusk.

Researching Toronto wildflowers along the Rouge
River, the train clattering on the overpass trestle,
we are walking down the embankment from Dennis
Street to Fortyfeet—our name for the Cummings
Canal—skirting the purple-blooming Scotch Thistle

And tiny white butterflies like starbursts. We are feeding
fish from our flour-webbed fingers, the black
water flowing from Ogle Estate, from rain, from deluges
out to the Atlantic, telling you how we named
our village before it was swallowed up in Georgetown

The City—Garnett parallel to Dennis Street
to the canal to Craig, John, William, Duncan Streets.
We come back to Craig. *My name! My name!* You say
the Cummings Canal not forty feet deep
but forty feet wide when they dug it—

Who, what? Whose fingers invade our dreams
consciousness, conversations on love, whose
slave labour allow us to float on cutout
car-top rafts like Huck Finn, and Jimmy and I

Narayan, Narayana, sun rising in the east over Fortyfeet
over Biscayne Bay, over the Clyde is the same
sun—Hay Surya, Hay Bhagwan—lighting our lips

Sheriff Street

Red dust rising when a car sped by
we stood on the government school platform
or watching from the unwindowed windows
girls bringing hibiscus and buttercups for dissection
in class. This is a stamen, this a pistil

Latchmansingh's three-wheeler disrupting a lesson
slipping into the canal after a drizzle
with a load of 100-pound sacks of flour.
What happened to the driver? They tarred the street
built a heavy duty bridge over the Cummings Canal

I couldn't picture daddy, a young man, hoisting
his polished Raleigh bicycle on his shoulder
walking west on Garnett Street to "the head"
then riding to Saturday evening shows at the Globe
or Stand or Metropole or Plaza or Astor all gone

The Chinese restaurants coming with the latest Cantonese
chow mein—not lo mein; look out for roaches for rats
and reconditioned Japanese cars flying by as on freeways

You returned to North America, after twenty years
Narine's Bakery still there, Narine gone, the second wife
still there on the other side multistoried hotels, drugs
fast food joints mimicking McDonald's, a laundromat
clubs—yes, a laundromat!—and a posh new whorehouse

Stealing Memory

These white polka dots on a blue summer
shirt are the saijan's blossoms against sky.
What? Tell me their name again, you say.
Drumsticks. *No, not that. What you said*
before. Saijan. It is raining all week
ever since we returned from Boston. One night.

The cats are fed. The dog scratches a sofa.
In Key West, tourists take pictures
outside Sloppy Joes's. You fancy the raindrops
are a typewriter's keys pounding 8.5 by 11
sheets as white as your blouse

When did the top buttons become undone?
An ivory nude on her stomach reading at night.
We were gay, then: one man, one woman laughing
in a Florida garden; we will not let anyone
patent our memory. You say: "*Come back to me*
My language. Come back to me, my love."

Remembrances

Not a one-legged dance in the dark
or maples in Toronto, not exclamations
under ceiling fans, or the ficus ficus
in Miami, the live oaks of everywhere

Not the squish on greenheart floors
or the coconut branches of Campbellville
not the full-bosomed monsoon squeal
or the pipal trees of Uttar Pradesh.
Nothing lives in memory anymore
Except that speck of ancient yogi-maya

My Father's Bubbles

The glass-topped pot boils
like a waterfall. We angle the cover
and get surf on a sugarbrown
beach—Georgetown's or Miami's?

Every pot makes its own percolation
and yet sounds the same. *Don't wash*
everything out, he said. Rinsing
chopped gill-baker* with lime.
It is years and even now
his concoctions permeate this kitchen

Steam rising from lava-thick surwa—
gravy, you say—infused with tomatoes
I, too, cook with no recipe.
Red fruits from Florida, channa

From California, jeera—cumin and
khari from India. No doubt our mothers,
real and step, made tasty dishes.
I remember nothing of our birth
mother's, who died too young

He was cooking since he was a boy,
Inez, my mother's cousin said—
Growing up across the street, we laughed.
A boy cooking! They were laughing still
at his wake. *Only girls cooked. But his stepmother*
when his father, your Aja, was away!
Working on the American airbase during WWII

* Gill-baker—an ocean fish

This channa curry—chole—can never taste
as good and yet will taste the same

as his kichari medley. The open pot
is an Atlantic-Kolkata-Ganga delta surf,
water on shells, deadfall: ancestral curry thumb

One Thousand

Bourbon went with Hapsburg or portraits
in oval frames. Perhaps, Marie Antoinette.
We were mesmerized by curls. Those years'
cravings ran to beers and twelve-year old
Demerara rums. No Johnnie Walker black or gold
no vodka or London gin on-the-rocks
was smoother. How explain voices
from childhood films? Shaken not stirred

We have no business being so beautiful.
Raleigh set out for El Dorado somewhere
in Guiana everyone in Elizabeth's court
had curls, we thought. We saw only hers, mommy
made waves in dark tresses, letting us watch

As the curlers locked—click, click, click—
in her friends' hair and hers. You smell
that lotion a thousand miles away, a thousand
years diving into the Atlantic, wet hair
emerging on her white shoulders. Men stared

Loved or lusted, who can say? Daddy's special
was Russian Bear Rum from D'Andrade's
rum shop that went under. He switched.
Turmoil in Europe and elsewhere. Napoleon
never made it to Moscow, nor Hitler, all that snow
no good for vegetarians. A fish bumpersticker

How could Van Gogh truncate smiles?
The merchant or the merchant's wife
starry nights, apples, sunflowers are
a thousand renditions, the waves of paint
on canvas making impressions. Freud or Oedipus

Pink heels peddling the Singer
The Magician of Lublin named his horse Shiva.
We moved yet again. Diasporas crossing
and re-crossing oceans in the same optic ship
there is no plain Jane, but how do you know
Bond was wrong? A thousand names for Vishnu
A thousand for you—shaken and stirred

Letters

Envelopes pile up. We are notices
we are bills, we are unwanted
advertisements and solicitations.

Ideas pile up. We are cancers
we are gamblers, we are the tells—
friends neglected in our obsessions.

Masterpieces pile up. We are the mirrors
of our ties, handheld supercomputers.
There are no letters. We have written none.

Searching for El Dorado

Perched on the Makouria'a bow on the Demerara
an Atlantic wind whipping hearts and skirts
making marriages in alcoves on upper deck and lower
deck on the sheltered stern on the vehicular cargo
bay between lorries and produce, you are Raleigh

Sailing up the Orinoco, but where the Golden City
Guiana Boy? Is there such a thing as English
Gold? Not in the Tudor's pudendum—pussymine
exploding. You take a chambermaid. Two coconut

Palms on the West Bank like eyes on a German
U-boat surfacing in the river's mouth searching
for Americans flying supplies from Atkinson*
Airbase across the Atlantic to Monty in Africa
a slave trade reversal. Ferguson shipbuilders

In Port Glasgow no longer a long way away.
We stand on steel fashioned by Scoti and Picti
sailing to this southern outpost of Empire
to deliver a steamer. What happened to Devi
seeking gold like Raleigh in Roanoke in Virginia
Elizabeth no longer patron, and finally in the Tower
A single blade, they said. I opt for double razors

* Originally an American airbase in Guyana (then British Guiana) during the Second World War, now the Cheddi Jagan International Airport

Brookline Beauty

Not because technology allows cameras
on phones, or because you glance away
afraid we may hold your eyes forever
in a digital screen: eight megapixels, ten
can't make a centurion's thighs
more taut under bouncing summer minis
or toes more firmly planted on suckerleafthin
sandals clutching the pave, no brighter light
on Beacon Street as we head for breakfast
ravenous after a short summer night

Summer Fire

Ringed by velvet trees, pines preferably
or spruce needles stuck together
fingers in glove like she who inhabited a hill
in Boston, Atlantic eyes are spring chlorophyll—
painted waves—a cottage in a college town
lined with books, barely glimpsing the Internet.

After seventeen years in the ground
cicadas overwhelm this dusk, crickets and beetles
and—O the mocking birds couldn't be far away!
and aren't, we'd grow old—no euphemisms—
together, never now, apart, apart, apart

I, General Giap[*]

Call me butcher, call me reckless

It was my duty to cleanse my land
of Legionnaires and Marines

If you come to my land with guns
that is how we welcome you

If you come to my land as tourist
that is how we welcome you

Call me anything, but call me patient—

Your Washington lost all his large
battles. So did I. Your Washington won
your war. So did I—mine

This alone will remain in our History Books.

* Giap—Vietnamese General credited with winning the Vietnam War

The Killing Fields of Sri Lanka

1

Take off all your clothes
the soldiers said, the old woman
recounts. Her voice disguised
on camera, her face concealed
in dark light. Fear in a TV feed
on the Internet? *They took all*
girls and young women behind;
they screamed and screamed
and then shots. We didn't find
their bodies, we didn't find the bodies—

2

You couldn't but for that thing
we cursed, that cancer stick we glue
to ears, ubiquitous soldiers' cellphones
doubling as camera for trophy videos
shot by jubilant soldiers, one focusing
on pudendum hairs of nude female bodies
strewn like slaughtered pigs on the ground.
Two soldiers hauling another naked corpse
by ankles, loading a truck tray and laughing
into the camera: "She has the best figure."

3

None had clothes. None. None. None.
None had breath. None. None. None.

4

You couldn't find their bodies
or the mass graves, you couldn't go back
you couldn't search—by order of the Lankan
military: No outside investigators allowed.
And no action by the UN. None. None. None

5

The last outsiders were UN staffers.
The pig-eyed ruler said: *We cannot guarantee*
The safety of the UN. He meant: We are going
to slaughter the Tamils. We want no outside
observers. We want no record, no pictures,
no evidence. He forgot in the Holocaust
it was Hitler's soldiers themselves who filmed
the carnage before and after the ovens: filmed
naked women running, then, their heaped jewelry

6

The Tamil women begged the UN staffers:
Please, don't go. Please, don't go, don't go.
There is no question, the staffer attesting—
evacuated and safe in England. He filmed the wails
the waving hands of women, the fingers of girls
poked through apertures in the UN compound fence
that one face through a fence-slat haunting
to the grave—

7

I have no camera to capture pain.
No power to order troops, no jets
to order airstrikes, no office to call
for an inquiry, no legal training to sue
for a war crimes trial. I have no voice.
Dead, I have no utterance, but yours

8

Where are your great writers, Lanka?
Where are your great painters and sculptors
your great poets—as poets speak only in poetry—
was that the "Homer of the Caribbean"?
These were no English patients recuperating
in an Italian villa, no sweet memory on celluloid
no Sikh bomb disposal expert clip at the Academy
of a love fest, a love lost, only a cardinal tweeting
in my flooded garden, the rain washing all away
except digital images: These are Tamil patients
shelled once, shelled twice, in a wooden school
converted to a hospital, and shelled yet again

9

We have no drugs, no medicines, no instruments
the hospital-in-a-school administrator says one day,
facing the camera. The following day, after the next
barrage, the camera faced him—on the ground
surrounded by women weeping over his shrapnelled corpse.

10

They did not *pass*. Not a poet in Ravana's court
or Rama's, I give you no euphemisms
no hyperboles. They were dead, dead, dead.

11

Two years later, rain falling
and crackling on the aluminum
of a Florida screenroom roof, you labour
like a great artist, with great attention
to rhyme and metre and grammar and taal
still smelling blood and curry through
the sliding door, see red plasma dripping on
corrugated zinc sheet, an unenclosed morgue

12

Red Cross, Red Crescent. The Lankan artillery officers
must have been thinking of Ashoka: time for a Red OM.
Fire a barrage on civilians—for concealed Tigers, no less.
Pause five minutes, ten. When relatives come out to tend
their wounded, to collect their dead, fire again
catching them in the open defenseless in mourning
wails drowning out the incoming whistle of shells

The fury of three or four or ten thousand years unleashed.
This is for helping Rama, for building Rama's Bridge—
Rama-Setu from Tamil Nadu to Lanka, for defeating
our Ravana come to life, reincarnated, Rajapaksha

a Singhalese manual: How to win a *civil* war. Ashoka
again. Victors do no wrong. In Colombo, all is well,
we play cricket in white flannels like gentlemen.

Execution of Bound, Blindfolded, Naked Tamils by Lankan Soldier

Forest green fatigued on sand coloured
with the ooze of arteries and veins
severed by bullets: you stand tall soldier
holding a gun above your intended's temple

You with the ten heads. You with the boon
of Shiva or Buddha. You with the Achilles heel
in your navel. You with a brother Vibhishana
shooting a trophy video on a cell phone

Laughing as you rooster-strut over
a nude Tiger sitting on a beach, blindfolded
hands back-bound. Bam! One shot behind
the head. Forest green fatigued soldier

Presidential-palaced Ravana, give up
with your commanders, said Rama

Your soldiers laughing over the naked-dead
female figures, one once a sari-clad Tamil
news anchor. Your ten heads are overdue
a tour of The Hague, or a World Court room
set up on the very sands you've made
The killing fields of Sri Lanka.

Le Repentir: Burial Grounds

1 Mommy

There, with queen palms roaring
they walled you in. Tombs and septic
tanks look alike. Worms feast in both.
Who gyrates in graveyards? Jumbies
and poets; both celebrate satanic verses.

2 Attacks from the Air: 9/11

This was not what the Vedantists
had in mind when they flew
into the skies, their Sanskrit scribes
and engineers recording to scale
replicas Germans created before
and during The War. Before those
Wrights. This was not what the Wrights
contemplated before Kitty Hawk.
There is no metaphor for murder.

3 Before and After

The casualties at Gettysburg are unsecret.
They were combatants. Not a civilian father
having his first coffee break of the morning.
Somebody's mother is somebody's daughter
just looking up from the morning numbers.
Smoke. Last words on a cell phone.

Today you ride a bike. You live in Toronto.
Today you ride a bike. You live in Tampa.
Today you always take the stairs.

How many bombs in Vietnam, or Japan?
One in Hiroshima. Just one in Nagasaki.
The count? You will never be popular.
Why is one more sacred than 3,000 than
40,000 Tamils—maybe 70,000—disappeared
in two weeks. There is no metaphor for murder.

Red Hanuman

We pour milk sweetened with honey—amrit
into a hole. Seven hands touching
the bamboo flagpole—it was what we had
but you could use wood, or steel—we lift
heave and stick the pole into moist earth

Red flag fluttering gaily in wind
red flag—or was that saffron—burning
on a battlefield, on Arjuna's pennant on an ancient
chariot, we celebrate your lighting up Lanka—
fire on your tail meant to curb your pride

That'll teach you, Ravana thought, laughing
in a Bollywood remake until you torched his capital
Colombo?—we rub dye—haldi—a turmeric paste
on the pole's green base seven times and seven times

Blood hued sindhur, dropping nutmeg into earth
and paan leaf, supari, a coin: A time capsule.
Until death do us part, we laugh. You are beating
clothes at the old washstand after guests depart

A standpipe in the jamoon shade
under the goldenapple's long branches nearby
red flag flapping in noon sun: bael
we tasted in the *Ramayana* before Hanuman
flew off to bring a mountain to the battlefield,
laye sajivan, the Leafoflife for wounded Lakshmana—

Bael again after friends and relatives depart.

The Devil Rides High

We come to save India
from the Kali blackness
a tongue extruded blood red
like the cardinal's robe
flaunted on the fence

The archbishop rides a mare
rides an ass in the jungle
or from Rome, or the heartland
of America private jets
for the Joshua Project,* the devil
rides high, higher than his Lord

* Joshua Project—An American Evangelical group, whose mission is to Christianize all of the world's peoples.

Sugar and Tea

Rolling down Darjeeling hillsides
this brew we sip in a spring café
overlooking green water clogged
with grounds from the land

Remnants and refuse from India
forgotten in the backwaters
of Florida, blackwater rivers and ponds
festooned by alligators waiting
to snatch an arm or leg or memory

Of child wandering down to watersides
black like handpicked leaves dried
from age and misuse unintentional

I have come from Kolkata, you still say,
Calcutta, to fertilize canerows, to weed dams
to reap canestalks'sharp cuts to manufacture
this sweetener I invented swirling

In china whose bones kneaded and baked
in dainty utensils as we look over oceans:
slavery didn't end with the end
of slavery, or the beginning of Indenture*

* With the end of slavery in the British West Indies (and elsewhere), more than 1 million Indians were transported from India to work the sugar plantations in slave-like conditions in the West Indies (including Guyana and Suriname on mainland South America), Fiji, Mauritius and other countries between 1834 and 1917.

Tea Drinking

No time to steep loose leaves
or restrain the swollen fragments
from floating in our mug.
Convenience deters a taste of one.
From where did this white thread
come and this teabag paper
from a longleaf pine or spruce?
hand dunking a satchel
in tepid water from a coffee machine

You are what you drink:
Essence from a cotton thread
a metal staple clasping string
hard hats taking down a tree
rubber wheels on freight trucks
running on Arabian fuel
the fingers plucking leaves
on hills in China or Kenya or India

To a Kashmiri Child in a Hindu Refugee Camp in Delhi

I would tell you—
Do not be so hasty
to join me—as if
you have a choice

As if you have a voice
in this New Delhi tent city.
What are your toys?
Not even a paper boat
to float in a puddle?

Your lakes are green—
grass or reeds or lilies.
Your birthright stolen
like the Tejo Mahalya
and the thinkers urge:

What is this sanitation
or cleansing in India
or upsetting balances!

You cannot go home again,
Yet, I would tell you:
Do not be so hasty to join me

Keeper of many homes
owner of none

Staff Trimming

Sweetgum, he said turning
to the glass wall and morning
sun on our shoulders. *Sweetgum*
not maples, he corrected. *You know*
how it goes. He didn't look up

Exiting the VP's office
a manager waiting as he gathered
his things. She accompanied him
to the exit. A moving picture train

They didn't use security guards
this time no explanations
except the whims of the new CEO
who could never be a pandit replaced.
Sweetgum, he said, and was gone.

Friday Prayers

You could have sent me into the river
and I would have gone. Who invented our calendar?
Being born on a Friday, they say. In a dusty album
we are sitting in front of the market crowd

In the mosque's shadow, we wash hands, face
knot kerchiefs on our heads: enter. How many times
I must touch head to ground immaterial
I would have done a thousand if you wanted
that evening after namaz, a full moon rising
on the Corentyne River, Surinam on the east bank
a lime green sliver, after the late show at the cinema

Tomorrow, a farewell photo in midmorning sun
smile shaded by a Castro cap. Toned thighs
short skirt, a call, a call if we wait for evening
I return to my city never, never the same again

*If Kali Were a Car**

If Kali were a car, not
the man from Nazareth
or the Prophet—which one
you ask hedging and fearing
a fatwah. Do Americans think
differently from the Raj
dying: the sun never setting
sets and an island calypso
ringing in your ears:
"Do the Dragon dance
Do the dragon dance . . . "
ting-a-ling-a-ling, ting-a-ling-a-ling
and, perhaps, another day
we can talk of another attribute
such as that blood tongue—keeper
of taste, but kali is not a car.
She is keepertime and timespace

* From Anne Waldman's 'Alpabeth of Mother Language'

ACKNOWLEDGEMENTS

Jude Barber & Louise Welsh for including "Campbellville" in the *Yonda Awa: Poetry from the Empire Café* (Glasgow, 2014, The Empire Café/Collective Architecture Ltd), and for making my visit to the UK possible—the touchstone for this collection.

The British Council: Catherine Muir, Sophie Wardell and the staff of the British Council for your hospitality and grace and for facilitating my visit to the UK.

The BBC: Razia Iqbal and especially Liza Greig for recordings and the publication of "Georgetown" in the BBC's fine Poetry Postcard series.

Cove Park, where the poems in the first part of this collection were written.

Dasun in which the following poems appeared in slightly different form: "Monsoon on the Fingers of God" (as "Indian Classical What"); "White Butterfly"; "Rain"; and "Remembrances."

The Edinburgh International Book Festival (Nick Barley, Catherine Campbell and many others for your warmth and for hosting readings at the EIBF), where some of these poems were written.

The Empire Café and all the wonderful people I met at/through the Café: Catriona Lexy Campbell (Scottish Writers' Centre); Chris Leslie and, especially, Denise Noone for very fine pictures—and many others. "Thanks" not enough.

The Saltire Society and staff (Alyson Thomas; Jim Tough, Sarah Mason) for hospitality, a wonderful reading space and for the chance to stand on cobblestones trod by RL Stevenson and his *Kidnapped* narrator.

Peter Nazareth, whose chance communication (and who will remind me there is no such thing as chance) made all of this possible.

South Asian Ensemble where the following poems appeared in various forms over several issues during the past four years: "Chalkboard"; "Horace on Poetry"; "This Life"; "Soul"; "Leaves";

"Stealing Memory"; "My father's Bubbles"; "One Thousand"; "Letters"; "Staff Trimming"; "Broomsticks at Alnwick Castle"; "Friday Prayers"; "If Kali Were a Car"; and "General Giap."

Ravi Shankar (1920-2012) who did for Indian classical music in the west what Swami Vivekanand, Paramahansa Yogananda, and BKS Iyengar did for yoga, and who inspired me to learn sitar and Indian classical music—the ancient system of improvisations of which (along with the improvisations on the dholak and pakhawaj and of taans, chowtals and other musical forms brought to the West Indies by Indian indentured immigrants) infuse my prose and poetry.

World Literature Today in which "Egret" and "Memoir: Mother of My Mothers" were published.

SASENARINE PERSAUD is an essayist, novelist, short-story writer, and poet. He is the author of twelve books: poetry collections, novels, and a book of short stories. He was born in Guyana and has lived for several years in Canada. He presently resides in Tampa, Florida.